AF881047

What Our Readers Have Said...

"Although I consider myself a seasoned sales professional, it is helpful to have past learning's refreshed. The books were also beneficial because of the information concerning 'trends' in the sales relationship. The sales process should be viewed as dynamic since business relationships change regularly."

•

"For the particular business I am in and the type of sales calls I have, I find that the books in the Pinpoint Sales Training Series are very often applicable to how I conduct business. I would recommend them to other sales people, just not ones that are in my industry."

•

"These books provide very good concepts. It fits in well with the Bell Leadership training program that I attended in November."

•

"I use this material in these books and apply it to my customers and other employees I work with."

•

"I would like to know other topics. Is there anything on Production Management or Consultative Selling or Time Management?"

•

"These books are great tools that should be used as guidelines for our everyday

supervisory practices. You need to take the time to do a short self-evaluation when reading them."

•

"The Pinpoint Training Series delivers information that could be used in a lot different areas."

•

"I like this because I can take them with me to read at a convenient time. I feel the little time I have to spend in the office is best use on activities that directly relate to revenue opportunities. I like the short amount of time it takes to keep up with these."

•

"I prefer the self-study approach; it fits in with my schedule."

•

"My thought is that the real value of these books comes into effect when doing the action plans."

•

"Short and sweet. These books are easy to comprehend."

•

"I have enjoyed reading these books. They are relevant to today's work environment and the ongoing change in the way we manage our workforce."

•

"I do feel that these books have been very helpful to me at my job."

•

"I think a lot of the recommendations in these books are very useful, and can be applicable to everyday situations. If nothing else, it's a good reference guide to fall back upon if a situation arises in the future."

•

"These books are relevant to today's work environment and the ongoing change in the way we manage our workforce."

•

Selling to Buying Groups

Pinpoint Sales Skill Development Training Series

TIMOTHY F. BEDNARZ

MAJORIUM
BUSINESS PRESS

Pinpoint Sales Skill Development Training Series
"Selling to Buying Groups"
Timothy F. Bednarz

Graphic design: Monika Pawlak

Majorium Business Press
2025 Main Street
Stevens Point, WI 54481
715.342.1018 • 800.654.4935

ISBN 978-1-882181-86-5

Printed in the United States of America

Introduction

The Pinpoint Sales Skill Development Training Series is designed for targeted training and education regarding increased improvement in a specific skill or competency.

Each book within this series is designed to be easy to use, understand and apply to your job. It can be used as a basis for training individuals, as a discussion guide or as a personal training tool.

Each chapter within this book discusses a specific concept. When you have completed all eight chapters you should have a 360° perspective of the topic.

Additionally, each chapter is divided into specific sections:

- The first section provides you with an overview of the topic
- The Implications section discusses why the concept is important, and why it is important to learn and apply.
- The Strategies, Tips & Techniques to Apply section teaches how to use and apply the particular concept to your work.
- The Points to Ponder section gives you something to think about or to be discussed with a group setting. These are questions not meant to be immediately answered, but to be pondered over time.
- The Training Activity section provides you with the tools to transfer what you have learned to your job. It is designed to help create an action plan to effectively apply the concept.

Each of the topics in this series is time-tested and proven in the marketplace. They have been used by thousands of employees as training tools. Many of the users have commented that what made these books valuable, was the ability to refer to them when a problem surfaced. They indicated that they remembered reading about the exact problem. They referred back to these books and found an appropriate solution.

You will find them equally valuable as a resource in your professional development library.

Table of Contents

LEARNING OBJECTIVES:

- To understand why selling to buying groups or committees are critical sales skills.
- To understand why more buying decisions are being made by groups and committees.
- To analyze the dynamics of a group.
- To identify the real decision makers.
- To develop a champion within a buying group.
- To effectively sell to groups and committees.

1

Adapting Sales Strategies to Group Decisions

With the downsizing and restructuring in the business world, more buyers feel at risk. They have learned that if a wrong decision is made, companies don't "shoot the messenger," but the buyer that listened to the messenger. As such, fewer buying decisions are being made by individuals: rather than take the risk, they shift the decision to a group, where the risk is diversified.

IMPLICATIONS – WHAT THIS MEANS TO YOU

The fact that companies are increasingly relying on buying groups and committees to make their purchasing decisions has many implications for salespeople to consider. Buying decisions take more time due to the group process. Additionally, the impact of the personal relationship with the individual buyer is diminished, although not eliminated. Finally, salespeople must learn to adapt their selling strategies to accommodate the needs of the prospect or customer in the way they buy.

Selling to buying groups takes a different set of skills. Salespeople must be better prepared, more informed and invest more time developing customer information before attempting to close the sale.

Additionally, salespeople must be more persistent than ever before—an area in which many fall short. Surveys have shown that many quit selling an account after 3 calls when it takes an average of 8 to 10 calls to land the sale.

STRATEGIES, TIPS & TECHNIQUES TO APPLY

As salespeople adapt their selling strategies to accommodate group decision making, there are several questions they need to address.

What is the Position of the Buyer?

One of the difficulties that many salespeople have in developing sales is identifying the decision maker. They cannot assume the person with whom they are dealing is the one entrusted with the final buying decision.

Unfortunately, decision makers are being increasingly shielded by a host of gatekeepers to prevent their time being wasted by countless salespeople. Consequently, most salespeople are dealing with individuals who, while they may be influencers, are not the decision maker.

Salespeople must assume that most buyers are part of a buying group or committee. Often many of these individuals are screeners, collecting data and forwarding it on for additional evaluation. Consequently, it is important for salespeople to understand exactly whom they are dealing with and their specific role in the decision making process.

Who Constitutes the Group?

A buying group or committee can consist of a group of employees from specific areas of the company or can be two business partners in a small company. Their purpose and structure can be as diverse as the companies the salesperson calls on. The makeup of most buying groups is seldom reflected on organizational charts, so it is important for salespeople to understand exactly who is on the committee and, if possible, the responsibility of each.

Who Is the Decision Maker?

When dealing with buying groups and committees, the identity of the ultimate decision maker is often shielded and protected. If salespeople are able to make a presentation in front of the group, the decision maker will be difficult to identify. They often linger in the background and listen to the discussions of the group. Many will take the group's decision under advisement; some will accept their recommendations.

While difficult, salespeople must take care to identify the ultimate decision maker. Without this critical information, sales to the group will be more difficult.

How Are Decisions Made?

Each company will make decisions differently. In some companies, the decision maker is in charge of the final decision; in others the recommendations of the group are final. Whatever the structure, salespeople must understand exactly how the buying decision is made. Without this critical information, they are literally selling in the blind, as they cannot shape a sales strategy that meets the informational needs of the group.

What Is the Decision Making Criteria?

Just as companies make decisions differently, each has an individual set of parameters that are used and applied. Salespeople must understand the criteria that are used in order to favorably position themselves against the competition.

POINTS TO PONDER — SOMETHING TO THINK ABOUT

1. How often are you experiencing buying groups versus individual buyers?
2. How have you seen buying decisions lengthen over the past several years?

TRAINING ACTIVITY — APPLICATION & ACTION PLAN

As you work with your prospects and customers, use the following key questions to develop strategies and additional questions that assist you to develop the information you need:

- What Is the Position of the Buyer?
- Who Constitutes the Group?
- Who Is the Decision Maker?
- How Are Decisions Made?
- What Is the Decision Making Criteria?

2

Selling to a Buying Team

In an effort to guard against making the wrong decision, more companies are requiring buying teams or committees comprised of a cross section of employees to sign off on major purchases. Doing so lowers the risk and spreads the liability for a wrong decision across the group.

IMPLICATIONS — WHAT THIS MEANS TO YOU

In some companies, teams are formally structured; while in others, they are so informal the company would never officially refer to them as a team. Salespeople should further understand that many companies and buyers are not particularly obliging and may do everything to place barriers in the salesperson's way to gain access to the buying team. This can be done for many reasons, but typically the individual members wish to remain free from a salesperson's influence or contact.

Selling to a buying team can be complex, but no more so than selling to an individual. Often it is the dynamics of the group that salespeople must understand. However, the biggest obstacle is often found in developing the information that allows salespeople to understand the structure and process of the buying team. While this often is time-consuming, once achieved, the process can move more quickly and smoothly.

STRATEGIES, TIPS & TECHNIQUES TO APPLY

Asking a prospect if they are the person who can authorize a purchase is not only ineffective, it is often insulting—particularly if the individual is not the decision maker. Salespeople must recognize that more buyers are soliciting input from others within their organization, and that many have far more influence than an outsider might imagine.

There are several stages salespeople must go through before they can fully comprehend how a purchasing decision is ultimately made.

Clarify the Team's Structure

When companies create teams, they're usually organized vertically. They are designed to assure that all the pertinent personnel are consulted on a purchase. Some teams are informal and can be difficult to comprehend since they can be created "on the fly."

Formal teams are easier to understand. It's clear to understand the reasons why someone is on the team. Additionally, how proposals are evaluated and who will make the final buying decision is usually part of the team's written charter. Often information on a formal team is easier to obtain since many will provide it as a service to their suppliers and vendors.

Who's in Charge

The simplest approach for salespeople to identify the decision making and influence structure is to ask the prospect or customer how he or she gathers information within the company. Determine who the buyer is consulting before a decision on the parameters of a product are specified and ask to interview these people. However, as simple as this approach may seem, it is often very difficult to achieve, since the identity of the decision maker is often shielded and protected.

Meet with the Buying Team

The salesperson's first responsibility is to identify the individual members of the buying team. Once the individuals have been identified he or she should request to meet with all involved.

During the initial meeting, the salesperson should go around the room and have each team member describe the three biggest challenges they are facing with their existing products and what they perceive to be the optimal solution.

Meet Individually with Each Team Member

Where possible salespeople should request individual interviews with each team member. These are excellent opportunities to involve product and technical support specialists to support the salesperson and be available to answer and address specific questions and issues.

Present the Most Cost-Effective Solution

This next team meeting is generally when the decision maker will make him or herself known, in either the first five minutes or the last five minutes of the meeting. He or she will typically stand up and say, "OK, I've heard all of this, and this is what I think we should do next."

Chances are salespeople will have already identified the decision maker at some point during the sales process. This will provide them with additional confirmation that they have identified the right person. If salespeople have adequately prepared themselves, the decision maker will tell them exactly what else they need in order to sign the order.

If salespeople have been unable to accomplish these steps or are still unclear as to what is going on in a prospect's business, they should interview some non-competitive salespeople to obtain inside information.

POINTS TO PONDER – SOMETHING TO THINK ABOUT

1. How successful have you been in identifying the decision maker (or decision-making structure) and selling to them (according to it)?
2. How have you overcome barriers to accessing the buying team?

TRAINING ACTIVITY – APPLICATION & ACTION PLAN

Develop research and sales strategies that allow you to identify the following:

- The use of a buying team.
- The identity of the buying team members.
- The structure of the team.
- The team's buying criteria.
- The identity and role of the decision maker.

3

Who Are You Selling To?

It is becoming more common for buying groups created from within a company to decide and determine the majority of meaningful purchases. Within this structure, group members are gathered together from various buying interests within the company. Most group members are directly impacted by the purchase and provide specific insights and perspectives. To facilitate good decision making, formal roles or tasks are either assigned within the group or understood by each member.

IMPLICATIONS — WHAT THIS MEANS TO YOU

Advanced selling techniques involve the ability of the salesperson to draw increasingly deeper distinctions during the sales process. The salesperson that is unaccustomed to dealing with buying groups is often confused as to who is really making the buying decision, which undermines the entire process.

It is essential for salespeople to understand that a failure to grasp the dynamics of group buying places them at a distinct disadvantage. The inability to understand the roles of the buying team results in an erosion of the salesperson's professional credibility, and rather than advance the sale, they will fumble through the process without any idea of what is actually unfolding.

STRATEGIES, TIPS & TECHNIQUES TO APPLY

Selling to buying groups can be complicated if not clearly understood. There are several different decision makers throughout the buying process and several different determinations that are made as a part of it. When salespeople understand the process, it is often easier to work through it in a logical sequence.

Salespeople need to comprehend that specific selling strategies must be employed to successfully sell at every level of the buying process. A "one size fits all" approach will not work in these situations. Strategies must be crafted to meet specific needs at each particular level.

One of the aspects of selling to large corporate buyers is determining the level of "people distinction." This is an understanding of the formal roles of the individuals involved in the buying process. These include the following major roles:

Evaluators

Evaluators do the legwork of determining available options and what major players (selling companies) have offerings in the marketplace. Evaluators are usually line managers from involved areas of company operations.

The evaluator is the primary contact person for most salespeople. However, many salespeople confuse the evaluator with the decision maker. This is because the role of the evaluator is to collect and filter as much information as possible for the buying group. They can act like a decision maker because they ask many questions and give the impression that the sale is moving forward.

While the evaluator is not the primary decision maker, he or she is an important influencer. If the salesperson does not sell this individual, it is unlikely he or she will be recommended to the next level. Since the evaluator not only collects but filters information for the buying group, he or she must be sold on the value of the offering.

Deciders

Deciders are the individuals who take the information gathered by evaluators and determine what they think the best option or options are for moving the purchase forward. Deciders usually rank as at least vice presidents in corporations.

In many buying groups, the decider can be the de facto decision maker. While their decisions may require authorization from a senior manager, many are automatically approved with a cursory review. However, the identity or the availability of the decider may be closely protected and screened in many corporations. Despite this, it is important for salespeople to contact these individuals since they make most of the critical buying decisions, based upon the input of evaluators and various buying group members.

Approvers

Approvers examine the decider's recommendation and make the final decision. Depending upon their individual style, the examination can either be casual or very intense. Approvers are ordinarily senior vice presidents or C-level executives (CEO, CFO, etc.).

Because the approver is the ultimate decision maker, many are extremely difficult to contact directly. However for the astute and persistent sales person, selling at the C-level can be very rewarding for a number of reasons, most notably, the lack of direct competition from other salespeople and the need to understand and speak in the terms and language used at those levels. Their thinking is strategic and involves the bottom-line impact on their business. They have little interest in the mundane details of features and benefits.

Influencers

Due to the accessibility problems many salespeople experience, the use of influencers is a valuable method to gain access to a buying group. Influencers may be at various levels of the corporate structure, but have the ability to influence decisions with their personal recommendations. While these are valuable resources for the salesperson to utilize, he or she should use an influencer to gain direct access to the various decision makers.

Champions

A champion is someone with influence who is either a member of the buying group or in authority outside of the group. The higher up in the organization, the more influence a champion can have.

In reality, a champion speaks for the salesperson, promoting his or her products and services and influencing others to agree with him or her. Additionally, a champion will provide the sales person with valuable information on how to sell to his or her company. Even with direct access to decision makers, salespeople should make all possible efforts to develop a champion.

POINTS TO PONDER — SOMETHING TO THINK ABOUT

1. What has been your success in identifying the various buying roles at a major or large corporation? Have you been stymied by an inability to identify the various roles? Explain.
2. Have you ever used different sales strategies to successfully sell to each level of decision making? Explain what has worked for you.

TRAINING ACTIVITY — APPLICATION & ACTION PLAN

1. Select several of the major accounts that you are currently working on. For each account identify the following:
    - Evaluator
    - Decider
    - Approver
    - Influencer
    - Champion
2. With the exception of the champion, you should be able to identify the specific individual that fills each role. A failure to do so indicates a need for additional information before you can sell this account.

4

A Failure to Adapt

The prevalent use of buying groups by most companies is a reality that most salespeople must deal with or face increasing levels of frustration. The use of a "one size fits all" solution and a lack of preparation contributes to this frustration.

IMPLICATIONS – WHAT THIS MEANS TO YOU

Selling to buying groups demands a higher level of sales sophistication than was required to successfully sell in the past. Salespeople must be more attuned to customized sales approaches linked with strong positioning strategies to effectively penetrate a buying group and achieve a positive outcome.

The use of outmoded sales techniques that present a fixed solution are wholly ineffective in the buying group environment. Companies are increasingly looking for customized solutions that meet specific needs and provide a guaranteed return on investment. Successful sales techniques demand adequate preparation, discipline and perseverance if the salesperson is to be successful. Selling to a buying group demands that salespeople build a strong relationship on multiple levels that extends beyond the actual sale.

STRATEGIES, TIPS & TECHNIQUES TO APPLY

A salesperson's failure to adapt can have appreciable consequences, none of which are favorable to the salesperson. Salespeople should recognize the incremental effects of using the wrong strategies when selling to a company that uses buying groups. These include:

False or Faulty Assumptions

Since it is a fact that most large organizations have shifted their decision making to buying groups, salespeople cannot make the assumption that they are identifying and dealing with a single decision maker. Many individuals will not reveal that a buying group is involved until it is time to make a decision, at which time it is often too late for a salesperson to get involved. Many individuals are prideful and want to be thought of and respected as the decision maker.

Even when the salesperson is dealing with a senior level manager, he or she will often defer the final decision to a group recommendation.

This is why during the qualification process it is essential to identify how a decision is reached, who is involved and the criteria that is to be used. Without this information, the prospect is not qualified, and this is the precise point at which problems will arise.

Wrong Person

When salespeople sell to a corporation using buying groups, the sales process must occur on multiple levels using various people with different roles in the buying group. It is not sufficient to just sell to an evaluator or an influencer. Nothing guarantees these individuals will work on the salesperson's behalf nor does the salesperson know the actual extent of their influence. Salespeople must use these individuals to leverage access to the key decision makers in the buying group and to gain vital information. They must sell to each of these individuals concurrently as opposed to sequentially in order to achieve results.

Wrong Focus

When salespeople work only with a single buyer without confirmation of their actual influence in the buying group, they can be easily led astray and create a focus that is inappropriate to sell the buying group. Within the group setting, salespeople who are selling across the group gain important insights and perspectives that allow them to formulate a clear definition of the needs of the group. This also allows them to influence a decision at many levels and from differing viewpoints. The selling principles are constant, but in the group setting they must be applied at various levels in differing degrees.

Wasted Time

Wasted valuable time is a damaging consequence of salespeople employing the wrong strategies when selling to buying groups. Selling to the wrong person with the wrong focus can result in the salesperson investing time and resources at the wrong point of impact. They can find at the time a decision is being made that they have not positioned themselves successfully within the buying group and have lost an opportunity to have their product or service seriously considered.

Lack of Results

The end result of salespeople expending a great deal of energy on the wrong person is that there is little or no likelihood of getting the sale. Without the knowledge gained by properly qualifying the prospect and the attention to strategically position themselves within the buying group, salespeople will find that all of their work will result in a loss of the sale.

POINTS TO PONDER — SOMETHING TO THINK ABOUT

1. Have you focused your efforts on a single buyer, only to lose the order to a decision made by a buying group?
2. How cognizant are you of dealing with more buying groups and less individual decision makers?

TRAINING ACTIVITY — APPLICATION & ACTION PLAN

1. Identify three or four major accounts where you feel you are "spinning your wheels".
2. Determine if any of the consequences listed above may be the cause of your problem.
3. If so, reevaluate your sales strategy and readjust.
4. If necessary, start over and properly qualify the prospect to identify how decisions are made, who is involved in the decision and the decision making criteria that they use.

5

Selling to a Buying Group

Selling to a buying group means that salespeople must understand both the psychology and dynamics of the group. It demands attention to detail and close observation of both the individual actions and reactions of a group member, as well as those of the entire group.

IMPLICATIONS – WHAT THIS MEANS TO YOU

Buying decisions are being increasingly made by groups rather than individuals. This is in large part due to the waves of downsizing experienced over the past decade: individuals became shell-shocked to the point of being fearful of making a decision. Often their jobs hinged on making the right decision, and rather than take the chance, more decisions were deferred to group consensus. The irony is that information technologies have made the flow of information more efficient, while the decision making process has slowed considerably.

Salespeople must be careful when selling to buying groups. Due to personal agendas and the internal politics of a company, the buying environment is full of potential dangers. It might take a consensus to make the sale, but it can take only one individual to undermine the salesperson's efforts.

STRATEGIES, TIPS & TECHNIQUES TO APPLY

Group dynamics and other factors beyond the salesperson's control come into play when dealing with buying groups. As previously mentioned, these can include personal agendas and internal power struggles. These factors, as well as alignment with an individual on the wrong side of a power struggle, can doom the sale.

The salesperson needs to be sensitive to the overall atmosphere of the group including any sense of anxiety, frustration or anger, which can be indicators of existing undercurrents that will impact the sale. If one segment of the group votes for the sale, the other can cancel it for no legitimate reason. In this instance the salesperson must be cognizant of what is occurring and address the needs of all members of the group in an attempt to build consensus despite internal differences. As an outsider, the salesperson cannot afford to alienate anyone and therefore must be sensitive to the group dynamics.

Adhering to the following guidelines can help ensure a successful outcome when selling to a buying group:

Dress Conservatively

The buying group's focus should be on the salesperson's presentation rather than his or her appearance. Rather than distract the group, it is advisable for salespeople to dress conservatively and professionally. *The Wall Street Journal* reported an incident where a saleswoman in a short skirt, spike heels and a see-through blouse made a disastrous presentation to a corporate board. Their recommendation was to avoid faddish and very stylish clothes during important meetings.

Introduce Yourself

Before the meeting starts, the salesperson should make sure to introduce him or herself to every member of the buying group. The salesperson should make mental notes of the individuals who seem to be enthusiastic about the meeting. This will be the initial core of supporters.

Remember Names

One of the most valuable tools salespeople have at their disposal is to remember everyone's name. The extra effort will not go unnoticed, as everyone appreciates having their name used. Some salespeople will either create a makeshift seating chart as they are introduced or place the business cards of the individuals in front of them as a memory key.

Do Homework

Before going into a group meeting, salespeople need to get information about the composition of the group they are presenting to. This will create the distinct advantage of being able to slant their sales presentation to the needs and issues concerning the buying group.

Identify the Group Leader

Every buying group has a leader, whether the official decision maker or an ad hoc group leader. They are identified by the way they control the meeting and hold the attention of the group. In many groups, the decision maker will stay in the background, carefully listening to what is being said and observing people's reactions. The identification of the group leader may not be obvious.

Identify the Devil's Advocate

Every group will have a devil's advocate or naysayer that will cause the most problems for the salesperson. It is important for salespeople to be able to clearly and concisely deal with this individual, including his or her problems and concerns. As such individuals can destroy the salesperson's chance for the sale, they should be handled carefully and their influence on the buying group not underestimated.

Identify Objections

Early in the presentation, salespeople should identify all of the objections and concerns of the buying group and write them on a flip chart or overhead. As the salesperson goes through his or her presentation, each should be specifically addressed and checked off. To maximize the effect of the presentation, before each objection is checked off, the salesperson should ask the group if that specific objection was addressed to their complete satisfaction.

Get the Group Involved

Salespeople should make their presentation as interactive as possible, asking questions, involving all members, soliciting answers and feedback from all group members.

Salespeople should pay attention to nonverbal communication and negative body language. They should actively involve the individual displaying the negative behavior to draw him or her out and uncover the reasons behind it.

Encourage Active Participation

Salespeople should involve the individuals they identified as enthusiastic during the introductions. Specific group members selling or advocating for the salesperson can have a dynamic impact on the group.

Address the Needs of the Group

Different individuals view and interpret information differently. Salespeople should recognize these individual differences by providing data and statistics for those who are comfortable with making decisions this way. They should also appeal to those who make their decisions emotionally.

Each group member is asking the question, "What's in it for me?" It's up to the salesperson to answer that question in a manner best suited to each individual group member.

Quality Handouts

The handouts salespeople provide to the group should be clear, concise and professional. They should lead the group step-by-step to a logical conclusion, or the salesperson's closing statement.

POINTS TO PONDER – SOMETHING TO THINK ABOUT

1. What problems have you observed selling to a group? Explain.
2. What strategies do you employ to successfully sell to a group? Explain.

TRAINING ACTIVITY – APPLICATION & ACTION PLAN

1. Select one company where you made a presentation in front of a buying group that did not end successfully.
2. Using the following items as a checklist, identify the potential causes of the problems you faced with the group.
3. Identify the lessons that can be derived from your analysis.
    - Dress conservatively
    - Introduce yourself
    - Remember names
    - Do your homework
    - Identify the group leader
    - Identify the devil's advocate(s)
    - Identify objections
    - Get the group involved
    - Encourage active participation
    - Address the diverse needs of the group
    - Create quality handouts

6

Working with a Champion

A champion is an influential member of the buying group or an individual who can strongly influence the buying group's decision due to their position within the company. The development and nurturing of a champion is an essential aspect of selling to a group or committee.

IMPLICATIONS — WHAT THIS MEANS TO YOU

In many group-buying environments, discussions and decisions are made without the presence or the benefit of the salesperson's input. It is not uncommon for salespeople to be denied direct access to the group to make a presentation, answer questions and correct any misperceptions there may be about their product or service. While there may be contact between the salesperson and individual members of the group, the salesperson is left out of the loop.

Salespeople should not underestimate the importance of developing and nurturing a champion. The champion believes strongly in the product or service being pitched and in essence represents the salesperson's interests in front of the buying group when they are not present.

STRATEGIES, TIPS & TECHNIQUES TO APPLY

The identification and nurturing of a champion can be a very important aspect of selling to a buying group. This individual can play several important roles in the buying decision:

Insight

A good champion will provide the salesperson insight about the inner workings of a buying group. He or she can inform the salesperson how the group works, who has the most influence and their personal agendas, the internal politics, what information to present and when, and a host of other important issues that the salesperson may not be aware of. Essentially, a good champion will teach the salesperson how to successfully sell to the group.

Feedback

A well-developed champion will provide the salesperson with valuable feedback on what is happening within the group, including other competitive offers being considered.

Influence

The champion will use his or her position and power to influence the group on the salesperson's behalf. He or she becomes the de facto representative of the salesperson in front of the group, or the "salesperson's salesperson."

While identification of a champion is not always possible, it is a critical aspect of selling to a buying group and should always be attempted.

Identification

The proper identification of a champion can be tricky. Many salespeople will identify someone who likes their product or service as a champion, but in fact has little or no influence within the buying group.

A good champion will be at a senior management level or someone who is well placed within the buying group. Salespeople must research and probe to identify these individuals. Once this is accomplished, they must take steps to convince them of the quality and value their product or service can offer his or her company.

One technique is for salespeople to identify the champion's hot button. Champions, like other individuals, want to know, "What's in it for me?" Salespeople can clearly answer this question by addressing the champion's hot-button issues, they can successfully accomplish this.

Development

Champions can be developed when salespeople use trust and rapport building techniques to create a personal relationship. The maxim "people buy from people they like," comes into play regarding champions. A good champion will like the salesperson and want to help him or her be successful. The interaction between a salesperson and a champion is similar to that of a mentor and a pupil. The champion is mentoring the salesperson through the buying process in his or her company. An attentive salesperson will listen closely and do whatever he or she is told.

Nurturing

Salespeople should continue to build and strengthen their personal relationship with champions and closely follow their directions. The champion is risking his or her reputation by supporting the salesperson, and they expect the salesperson to act in a way that supports his or her actions. If the salesperson fails to follow the champion's instructions or attempts to circumvent them by short-circuiting the process, he or she will feel betrayed. Once the trust is betrayed, the salesperson has lost his or her champion. He or she will not risk their reputation on the salesperson again.

Follow-Up

Whether or not the salesperson is successful in getting a sale from the buying group, he or she must follow up and maintain the relationship with his or her champion. Failure to do so will make the champion feel he or she was used for the salesperson's personal gain. Since the future is always uncertain, the salesperson will never know when they may need the services of his or her champion. Worth its weight in gold, the relationship should be continued, developed and nurtured.

POINTS TO PONDER – SOMETHING TO THINK ABOUT

1. How successful have you been in using champions in the past?
2. What techniques do you use to identify potential champions, and how do you nurture them?

TRAINING ACTIVITY – APPLICATION & ACTION PLAN

Identify strategies and techniques that can be used to develop and nurture a champion:

1. Determine at which level a champion should be in a company.
2. Ascertain ways to identify potential champions.
3. Create an initial approach to a potential champion.
4. Determine how to effectively develop a potential champion.

7

Developing Group Decisions

When selling to buying groups, salespeople must use the art of persuasion to gain both agreement and consensus from all members of the group. Hard selling and manipulative sales tactics are not effective and in fact can be a fatal mistake.

IMPLICATIONS — WHAT THIS MEANS TO YOU

The use of persuasive selling techniques is most helpful to reaching group decisions because it develops a healthy dialogue and a positive debate about the value and merits of a salesperson's product or service. If salespeople use manipulative techniques, it exposes their intentions and personal focus while making the process a competitive game.

This is important for salespeople to understand because when dealing with the dynamics of a group, many of the older and more traditional selling methods are not effective. It takes the understanding of group psychology and the use of methods and strategies that address the individual and total needs of the group.

STRATEGIES, TIPS & TECHNIQUES TO APPLY

Selling to a buying group means that salespeople must seek both an agreement and consensus of the group to buy. As previously mentioned, this is often complicated by group dynamics, personal agendas and internal politics. This involves techniques that salespeople can employ that persuade the group and bring them to the salesperson's point of view. This is accomplished in the following manner:

Credibility

For a sale to be achieved in the best of circumstances, the prospect or customer must make a leap of faith. When salespeople are selling to a buying group, they encounter individuals in varying stages of commitment. Some are willing to make the commitment, some can be easily persuaded, others are highly resistant.

The initial barrier that salespeople must overcome with groups lies in the establishment of credibility on two levels. The first regards the salesperson's personal credibility. This includes the perception of the salesperson's honesty and trustworthiness, and is based on their personal appearance, words and actions.

The second level concerns the salesperson's professional credibility. Without professional credibility, which is evaluated by the use and application of the salesperson's knowledge and expertise, their insights and recommendations to the group will have no validity.

Once salespeople have established credibility on both levels, they have positioned themselves to successfully sell to the group.

It should be noted that one-on-one relationship building is recommended where and when possible. If the salesperson can personally interact with each member of the group, they not only build trust and rapport, but also insight and understanding into the motivation of every individual member.

Common Ground

One of the key concepts of selling and persuading a group is to achieve common ground. This means that the salesperson needs to address each group member's self-interest. If the salesperson's message does not sufficiently address "what's in it for me?" for each member of the group, it will fall on deaf ears.

This is why adequate preparation is required so that salespeople can clearly understand each member's viewpoint and then address it within the confines of their presentation.

In addition to common ground, salespeople must also search for shared ground. These are areas of mutual agreement between the salesperson and the group. This allows salespeople to approach the group from the perspective of shared and mutual concern. This gives salespeople a starting point of agreement and a foundation on which to build the rest of the presentation.

Compelling Arguments

The establishment of credibility and mutual interests gives salespeople a good foundation to bring the group to both agreement and consensus. This is done by the use of compelling arguments, substantiated with documentable facts. The first two steps build the connection to the group. Through pure sales presentation skills the salesperson is able to sell the group on the value of the purchase. However, there is one key difference: the sales presentation must address the individual self-interests of each member.

Commitment

Selling to buying groups is not for salespeople concerned only with earning a commission. It is a pure form of consultative and customer focused selling that demands a commitment from the salesperson to the needs of the customer. The use of buying groups is typically reserved for large ticket purchases and to qualify suppliers and vendors for long-term relationships. The level of personal and professional commitment made by the salesperson is closely related to the levels of credibility established within the group.

Additional Factors

Salespeople should be aware of several techniques when selling to a group. In many instances, the buying decision keys on several dominant members of the group, and the rest of the group will tend to agree with what they have decided. This is not to say these individuals are the decision makers, but that their personalities tend to dominate and influence the entire group.

When salespeople encounter dominant personalities in a group setting, they need to focus on these individuals and satisfy them. It is readily apparent who these individuals are since they will be the most vocal and controlling members of the group.

Finally, salespeople should employ consensus building techniques throughout their presentation, always seeking agreement and consensus before moving on to the next point, then summarizing all points of agreement at the conclusion of the presentation.

POINTS TO PONDER — SOMETHING TO THINK ABOUT

1. What types of selling techniques have you used to persuade buying groups?
2. What selling techniques have you used that are ineffective in selling to buying groups?

TRAINING ACTIVITY — APPLICATION & ACTION PLAN

1. Perform a self-analysis of the factors that establish your credibility. Rate the perceptions that each of the following factors generate:
    - Personal appearance
    - Use of language
    - Clothing
    - Tone and tempo of your speech
    - Professional knowledge of customer, product and competition
    - Level of personal expertise
2. Identify specific ways to change any negative perceptions that could damage your credibility.

8

The Hidden Decision Maker

Within the confines of a buying group resides a single member who wields the power to approve or deny the sale. The other members of the group may provide feedback and insights, but the final authority rests with this individual. However, it is not easy to identify this individual; in fact many prefer to be screened or masked from outside buying influences in order to be able to make a more objective decision.

IMPLICATIONS – WHAT THIS MEANS TO YOU

The hidden decision maker or dealmaker is the key member of any buying group and where the ultimate authority to make the purchase lies. Consequently it is critical for salespeople to not only identify this individual but also to successfully sell them.

Additionally, salespeople must recognize that the internal politics of the organization or this individual's personal agenda can influence his or her decision.

This is important for salespeople to understand not only because of the power the decision maker possesses, but also due to the fact that even if this individual is successfully identified, it may be difficult to sell to them due to the internal politics and personal agendas that may be brought into play. Therefore, as the key to the sale it is equally important for salespeople to develop a clear understanding of what is motivating this individual.

STRATEGIES, TIPS & TECHNIQUES TO APPLY

Salespeople must identify the hidden decision maker or dealmaker in order to successfully sell to a buying group. This often is not as easy as it may seem, since job titles and positions in an organizational chart are not always the most reliable indicators of the true power and influence of this individual. Therefore it is important that salespeople understand how to define and identify a hidden dealmaker by understanding the following characteristics:

Position

The position of the hidden decision maker is derived from his or her influence and credibility with C-level executives (CEO, CIO, CFO, etc.). Because of their influence and power within the organization, the outcome of the entire sale is based upon the salesperson's success in both identifying and motivating this individual to buy. Due to their position both in the company and the buying group, when they talk, the rest of the group listens.

Characteristics

While a decision maker or dealmaker may wish to remain anonymous, there are certain characteristics and behaviors that provide clues to the identity of this individual. The key characteristics of the hidden dealmaker that salespeople should look for includes:

- Access to senior management
- Involvement in other major projects
- Has the most to gain from the decision
- Understands the corporate goals and objectives
- Has influence over the buying group
- Has a high degree of self-confidence and self-assurance
- Has a strong ego and desires authority

Power

Within many buying groups, certain members will have the power to veto a purchase from a specific vendor. However, they lack the authority to approve a purchase on their own. Typically the hidden decision maker will have the authority to either approve or veto a sale.

Influence

The personal levels of influence for a hidden decision maker or dealmaker will obviously vary from company to company and from person to person. Their influence may extend to senior management, or they may have the power to change the opinions of other members of the buying group.

Expertise

The hidden dealmaker may be a recognized technical expert within the company. This is especially true in technological sales.

In other instances, the dealmaker would be the user of the proposed product or service and therefore able to recognize the value of the offering.

It should be noted that the hidden decision maker could be a member of senior management or a trusted advisor. In all instances, this individual has the authority and expertise to either recommend or make the purchase.

POINTS TO PONDER — SOMETHING TO THINK ABOUT

1. How successful have you been in the past in identifying the decision maker or dealmaker within a buying group?
2. Once you have identified a dealmaker, how successful have you been in uncovering their personal motivation and crafting a solution accordingly?

TRAINING ACTIVITY — APPLICATION & ACTION PLAN

1. Select a buying group that you have recently sold to or are currently working with.
2. On a sheet of paper create a graphic representation of the group.
3. Based upon your observations:
    a. Assign roles and responsibilities to each member.
    b. Identify the authority to either approve or deny the sale.
    c. Identify the interrelationships between individual members.
    d. Plot the flow of both power and influence between individual members.
4. Based upon your analysis, determine if this provides a better understanding of the dynamics of the group.

About the Author

Timothy F. Bednarz, Ph.D. is CEO of the American Management Development Group, Inc. For over 20 years he has researched, designed and authored hundreds of learning and development programs used by Fortune 1000 companies.

He is also the author of *Great! What Makes Leaders Great. What They Did, How They Did It and What You Can Learn from It* (2011).

Speaking Availability

Timothy F. Bednarz, Ph.D. is available for speaking engagements for your next meeting or association event. He can be contacted at 800-654-4935 or by e-mail at timothy.bednarz@majorium.com.

Bulk Sales

Bulk sales of this book or any other titles available from Majorium Business Press. Inquiries can be directed to sales@majorium.com, or by phone at 800-6654-4935.

Quick Order Form

Fax orders: 715-342-1118. Send this form.

Telephone orders: Call 800-654-4935 toll-free. Have your credit card ready.

Email orders: sales@majorium.com

Postal orders: Majorium Business Press, 2025 Main Street, Stevens Point, WI 54481, USA.

Please send the following books:

____

____

____

____

Please send more FREE information on:

❑Catalog ❑Speaking/Seminars ❑Mailing Lists ❑Consulting

Name: ____________________________________

Address: __________________________________

City: __________________ State: ____ Zip: _______

Telephone: ________________________________

Email address: _____________________________

Sales tax: Please add 5.5% for products shipped to Wisconsin addresses.

Shipping by air:

United States: $4.00 for first book and $2.00 for each additional product.

International: $9.00 for first book; $5.00 for each additional product (estimate).

Made in United States
Cleveland, OH
06 November 2026

47678343R10026